Flavour

HERTFOR

RECIPES

Compiled by Julia Skinner

THE FRANCIS FRITH COLLECTION

www.francisfrith.com

First published in the United Kingdom in 2011 by The Francis Frith Collection®

This edition published exclusively for Identity Books in 2011 ISBN 978-1-84589-573-0

British Library Cataloguing in Publication Data

Flavours of Hertfordshire - Recipes
Compiled by Julia Skinner

The Francis Frith Collection
Oakley Business Park,
Wylye Road, Dinton,
Wiltshire SP3 5EU
Tel: +44 (0) 1722 716 376
Email: info@francisfrith.co.uk
www.francisfrith.com

Printed and bound in Malaysia

Front Cover: **BISHOP'S STORTFORD, WINDHILL 1909** 61337p
Frontispiece: **HITCHIN, ST MARY'S CHURCH FROM MARKET PLACE 1908** 60881

The colour-tinting is for illustrative purposes only, and is not intended to be historically accurate

CONTENTS

In the 1930s, 40s and 50s market gardening was a hugely important industry in Hertfordshire. The fine quality of the silty soil in the valley of the River Lea in particular in the south-east of the county was ideal for the production of vegetables and soft fruit and a wide range of crops was grown, including strawberries, carrots, cabbages, cucumbers, tomatoes, Brussels sprouts, lettuces and peas – hundreds of people would arrive to help with the pea picking as itinerant workers in the 1930s.

WALTHAM CROSS, FOURE SWANNES HOTEL 1921 70173

RECIPE

CREAM OF CUCUMBER AND GREEN PEA SOUP

Hertfordshire's market gardening tradition had early origins – in 1824, J C Loudon described the extensive production of cucumbers in the county in 'An Encyclopaedia of Gardening – Comprising the Theory and Practice of Horticulture, Floriculture and Arboriculture': 'In Hertfordshire, whole fields are annually seen covered with cucumbers … the produce of which is sent to the metropolis for pickling'. Cucumbers remained an important crop in the Lea Valley of Hertfordshire until the mid 20th century – the Rochfords in the Turnford/Cheshunt area were particularly famous for cultivating cucumbers in great numbers. This soup recipe combines cucumber with several of the other vegetable crops that the county was famous for in the past.

> 1 cucumber, about 450g/1 lb in weight
> 1 onion, peeled and chopped
> 1 large carrot, trimmed and sliced
> 900ml/1½ pints chicken or vegetable stock
> 450g/1 lb green peas, fresh or frozen
> 25g/1oz butter
> Salt and freshly ground black pepper
> A little freshly grated nutmeg
> About 150ml/ ¼ pint single cream, to finish
> Finely chopped fresh chives or parsley to garnish

Cut the unpeeled cucumber in half lengthways, scrape out the seeds and chop it into small pieces. Melt the butter in a large saucepan, add the chopped onion and cook gently for about 5 minutes until it is soft and transparent. Add the carrot, cucumber, and peas, and cook for a further five minutes. Add the stock and nutmeg and bring to the boil, then reduce the heat, cover the pan with its lid and simmer for 30 minutes. Remove from the heat and allow to cool a little, then process the soup in a blender or liquidizer.

When ready to serve, add the cream to the soup and heat through, but do not allow the soup to boil. Season to taste with salt and freshly ground black pepper. Serve in individual bowls with a swirl of cream on the top and a garnish of finely chopped chives or parsley.

RECIPE

WATERCRESS SOUP

An important crop grown in Hertfordshire in the past was watercress, particularly around Hemel Hempstead and Berkhamsted. About one sixth of the total output of watercress in the country used to be produced from the watercress beds of the River Gade and its principal tributary, the Bulbourne. The industry around Hemel Hempstead survived until 1947, when water was diverted from the River Gade to supply the New Town of Hemel Hempstead with water. The altered course of the river was also used to create the Water Gardens as a focal point for the New Town, a feature of which is the delightful Rock and Roll Statue of a couple dancing (shown opposite), which was placed there in the 1960s. Watercress is still grown on a small scale in Hertfordshire, for instance by the Nine Wells Watercress Farm at Whitwell, near Hitchin, which sells its produce at local farmers' markets and farm shops. Traditionally-grown watercress is a super-food packed with nutrients, with a distinctive peppery, slightly bitter, flavour. In this recipe it is used to make a delicious soup.

> 50g/2oz butter
> 2 bunches of watercress with their stalks removed, washed and
>   chopped (but reserve a few sprigs to garnish the soup)
> 1 medium onion, chopped
> 25g/1oz plain flour
> 600ml/1 pint milk
> 450ml/ ¾ pint chicken or vegetable stock
> 6 tablespoonfuls single cream

Melt the butter in a large pan, and gently fry the watercress and onion for a few minutes until softened. Stir in the flour and cook for a further one minute. Slowly stir in the milk, a little at a time, and then the stock. Bring to the boil, stirring all the time, until thickened, then cover and simmer gently for 30 minutes. Remove from the heat and cool for a few minutes, then liquidize. Before serving, add the cream and reheat gently, taking care not to allow the soup to boil. Serve in individual bowls with a swirl of cream and a sprig of the reserved watercress leaves to garnish.

HEMEL HEMPSTEAD, THE ROCK AND ROLL STATUE AND THE WATER GARDENS c1963 H255041x

5

HERTFORD, FORE STREET 1922 71852

HARPENDEN, THE VILLAGE 1897 39730v

Jane Austen's famous novel 'Pride and Prejudice' is set mainly in Hertfordshire. Some scholars think she fictionalised Hertford as 'Meryton' in the book, in which case 'Longbourn', the home village of the Bennet family, might be Ware. However, Dr Kenneth Smith of Buckinghamshire New University at High Wycombe put forward an alternative theory in his essay in issue 27 of 'Persuasions', the journal of the Jane Austen Society of North America, suggesting that 'Meryton' is Harpenden, 'Longbourn' is Redbourn, and 'Netherfield Hall', home of Mr Bingley, is Kimpton Hall (see: www.jasna.org/persuasions/printed/number27/smith.pdf). An important scene in the book is the ball at Netherfield Hall. Mr Bingley says of it: 'As for the ball, it is quite a settled thing; and as soon as Nicholls has made white soup enough I shall send round my cards'. White Soup is a delicate broth made with white meat and stock, almonds, cream and eggs which became very popular in the Regency period as a dish to serve at balls and suppers. The recipe is given on the opposite page. Nowadays it would make an ideal soup for a dinner party, especially if you want to impress your own Mr Darcy…

RECITE

WHITE SOUP

White Soup was traditionally made with veal stock and meat, but this recipe follows Mrs Beeton's example and uses chicken stock and meat instead. It is an excellent way of using leftover cooked chicken, especially if you have made stock from the carcase – otherwise use the best quality chicken stock you can find. Another ingredient of White Soup is almonds. Pounded (or ground) almonds were often used in the past as a thickening ingredient for sauces or soups, or to lighten cakes and puddings. This is a much-simplified version of the old recipe – modern kitchen equipment means you no longer have to pound the chicken and almonds to a paste in a pestle and mortar, or sieve the soup through muslin to make it smooth. This amount serves 4-6.

1.2 litres/2 pints good chicken stock
50g/2oz ground almonds
75g/3oz cooked chicken, chopped into small pieces
A little extra chicken to garnish, very finely diced
1 slice good white bread, crusts removed
Grated zest of 1 lemon
A pinch of mace or nutmeg
2 raw egg yolks
150ml/ ¼ pint double cream

Bring the stock to the boil in a large saucepan. Crumble the bread and add it to the stock with the chopped chicken, ground almonds, lemon zest and mace or nutmeg. Bring back to the boil, then reduce the heat and simmer very gently for one hour. Remove from the heat and allow to cool a little, then process the soup in a blender or liquidizer until it is very smooth. Return to the cleaned pan. When ready to serve, mix the egg yolks with the cream and a little of the soup liquid, then add to the pan. Bring the soup to the boil, stirring all the time, until the soup has thickened slightly. Season to taste with salt and pepper and serve immediately, with a garnish of a few finely diced pieces of chicken.

RECIPE

TOMATO CHARLOTTE

In the first half of the 20th century, market gardening was a hugely important industry in Hertfordshire. The south-east of the county was an almost limitless expanse of glasshouses, and many new techniques for growing crops under glass were developed there. Until quite recent times tomato growing was particularly important in the Lea Valley, especially around Cheshunt, but rising costs, particularly of fuel, caused all but the most efficient growers to give up. However, some of the remaining growers are investigating modern energy-saving methods, and locally-grown tomatoes are still produced in the county, although no longer in the huge amounts of former times. This is not a traditional Hertfordshire recipe for tomatoes, but was a popular way of serving them in the past in the Home Counties, and is given here as a way of celebrating the important role of tomatoes in Hertfordshire's food history. It is an unusual and tasty way of serving tomatoes as a vegetable side dish or light supper dish, and the basil and sugar really bring out their flavour.

> 450g/1 lb tomatoes, skinned and sliced
> 2 teaspoonfuls caster sugar
> 1 tablespoonful chopped fresh basil leaves
> Salt and freshly ground black pepper
> 115g/4oz fresh white breadcrumbs
> 50g/2oz butter

Pre-heat the oven to 180°C/350°F/Gas Mark 4.

Place a layer of sliced tomatoes in a buttered ovenproof dish. Season with a little salt and pepper, and some of the sugar and chopped basil leaves. Cover with a thin layer of breadcrumbs, and dot with small pieces of butter. Repeat the layers, plus the seasoning, until all the ingredients have been used up, finishing with a layer of breadcrumbs and butter. Bake in the pre-heated oven for about 30 minutes, until the top is crisp and golden brown.

RECIPE

POTATO AND CHEESE CAKES

Little Gaddesden near Tring was the home in the 18th century of the farmer and writer William Ellis. He detailed a number of farming practices and recipes from 18th-century Hertfordshire in 'The Country Housewife's Family Companion' of 1750 (republished by Prospect Books in an enlarged facsimile edition in 2000). He was particularly keen on cultivating potatoes, which at that time were not widely grown in southern Britain. He wrote of the potato: 'This is a most serviceable and most wholesome root, because it is of a nourishing satiating nature, and admits of being eaten in several shapes; as with bacon, pickled pork, salt beef, mutton, salt fish; in pyes, in puddings, with butter, or with milk &c. &c. And as they are easily propagated, no farmer, labourer, yeoman, nor gentleman, should be without them, as they value their pockets...'. These cheese and potato cakes make a tasty breakfast or supper dish.

> 450g/1 lb potatoes, peeled
> 25g/1oz butter or margarine
> 1 rounded teaspoonful dry mustard powder
> 150g/5oz hard cheese of choice, finely grated
> Salt and pepper
> 1 egg, beaten
> A little plain flour, to flour your hands
> Oil or dripping, for frying

Cook the potatoes in boiling salted water for 15-10 minutes until they are tender. Drain the potatoes then mash them with the butter or margarine. Add the mustard powder, cheese, beaten egg and salt and pepper to taste, and combine the mixture well. Flour your hands and form the mixture into about 8 small cakes, and flatten them slightly. Heat the fat or oil in a frying pan and fry the potato cakes on a gentle heat for a few minutes on both sides, until they are golden brown. Alternatively, the potato cakes can be cooked on a greased baking tray in the oven, for about 15 minutes at 200°C/400°F/Gas Mark 6.

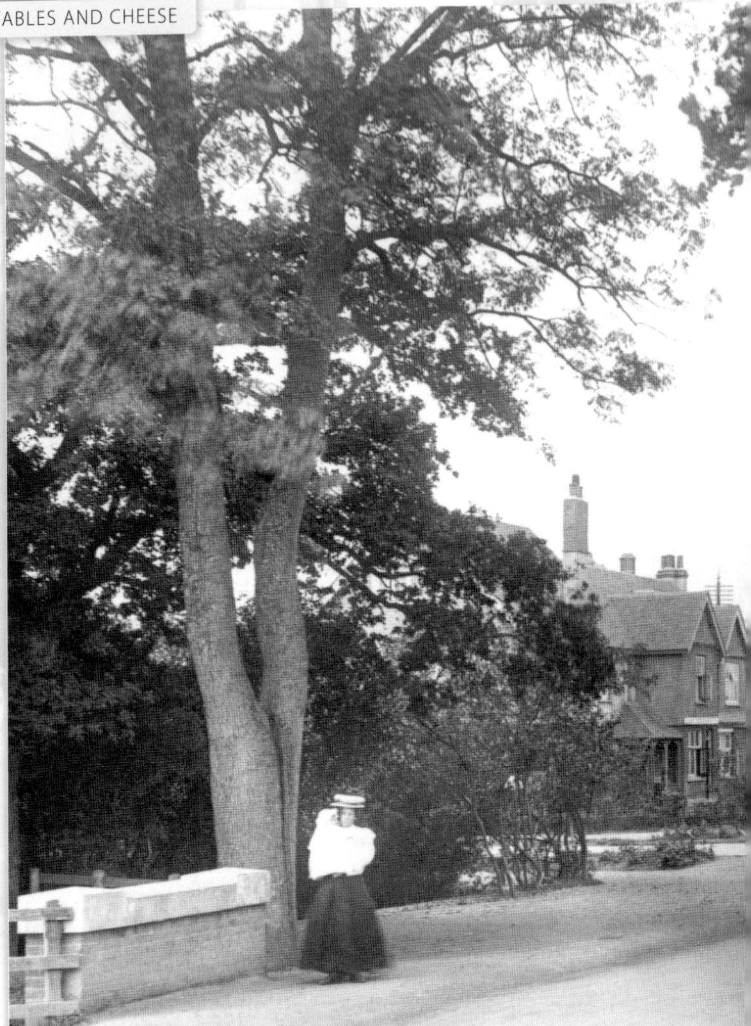

LETCHWORTH, BIRDS HILL CORNER 1908 60884

CHEESE AND PEARS...

There are several artisan cheesemakers in Hertfordshire nowadays producing excellent goats' milk cheeses. Wobbly Bottom Farm near Hitchin (www.wobblybottomfarm.co.uk) makes a wide range of interesting cheeses from the milk of cows, sheep and goats, including their Blue Goat Cheese, Goat Cheese with Nettles, and the intriguing Monks Revenge, which they describe as 'a very strong goats' cheese full of flavour'. Another famous producer is Elizabeth Harris on the Childwickbury Estate near St Albans, who makes goats' cheese in two varieties – Childwickbury, a smooth, fresh goats' cheese available for sale 24 hours after making, and Verulamium, named after the old Roman town at St Albans (see page 16), which is a matured cheese with a more pronounced flavour. Both are sold at the weekly Saturday market in St Albans, on the cheese stall outside the 'Monsoon' shop, and at the 'Buonjourno Italia' delicatessen in Lattimore Road in St Albans, as well as the Neals Yard Dairy shops in Borough Market and Covent Garden in London. In the recipe on the opposite page, goats' cheese is used in a classic combination with Conference pears to make a savoury tart ideal for a summer lunch or to take on a picnic.

The Conference pear was developed at the famous Rivers Nursery in Sawbridgeworth in east Hertfordshire, believed to have been the location of the first fruit farm in England, which was founded in 1725 by John Rivers. The Conference pear is a dessert variety with juicy, sweet flesh but it can also be served poached or lightly stewed and makes a good culinary pear. It was first sold a hundred years before the Rivers Nursery closed in 1985, and was so named because when it was exhibited at the International Pear Conference in Chiswick in 1885 it was awarded the only first-class certificate of the event, and the judges asked for it to be named in honour of the occasion.

RECIPE

SAVOURY GOATS' CHEESE AND PEAR TART

If you don't like goats' cheese you can use a tangy blue cheese in this recipe instead, such as Stilton cheese, which goes very well with the pears.

> 225g/8oz plain flour
> 115g/4oz butter or margarine
> Salt and freshly ground black pepper
> 3-4 Conference pears, depending on size
> 3 eggs
> 300ml/ ½ pint milk
> 250g/9oz goats' cheese (or Stilton cheese, if preferred)
> 12 walnut halves, chopped into small pieces

Pre-heat the oven to 200°F/400°F/Gas Mark 6, and grease a flan dish about 22-26cms (9-10 inches) in diameter. Sift the flour into a mixing bowl with the salt. Rub in the fat. Add enough cold water to mix to a firm dough, and knead lightly until smooth and elastic. Roll out the dough and use it to line the flan tin. Prick the base all over with a fork, place a piece of greaseproof paper with some baking beans on the pastry base, and bake blind in the pre-heated oven for 10 minutes. Remove the beans and paper, and return to the oven for a further 5 minutes to dry out the base. Reduce the oven temperature to 180°C/350°F/Gas Mark 4.

Peel the pears, cut into quarters lengthways and remove the core sections. Arrange the pears in the pastry case. Whisk the eggs and milk together, and season to taste with salt and freshly ground black pepper. Pour the mixture into the pastry case. Cut the cheese into small pieces and arrange over the top, plus any crumbs. Sprinkle over the chopped walnuts. Bake in the centre of the oven at the reduced temperature for 30-40 minutes, until the filling is risen and firm to the touch. Leave the tart to cool a little and settle, then eat it warm, or otherwise eat it cold.

St Albans in Hertfordshire is named after St Alban, Britain's first Christian martyr, who lived in the 3rd century AD in the Roman town of 'Verulamium' that stood in the area of Verulamium Park in the modern city. The Verulamium Museum in the park holds a fascinating collection of Roman finds, including a fine mosaic floor. On the western outskirts of St Albans at Bluehouse Hill are the remains of the unique Roman theatre of Verulamium. The only example of its kind in Britain, this was a theatre building with a stage, rather than an amphitheatre.

St Alban gave shelter in his Verulamium home to an itinerant Christian priest, and, impressed by his teachings, converted to Christianity himself. However, this was a time when Christians were persecuted in the Roman Empire, and eventually he was arrested. After refusing to make offerings to the Roman gods and stoutly affirming his Christian beliefs, he was led out of the city to a hillside where he was beheaded for his faith. Pilgrims began to visit the martyrium soon after St Alban's death, and the martyrium subsequently grew into a monastic community that was refounded around AD793 by the Anglo-Saxon King Offa of Mercia, giving St Albans its name and a Benedictine abbey where the saint's remains were housed in a shrine. Construction of the present abbey church at St Albans began in 1077, and by the 12th century St Albans Abbey was the premier abbey of England. After the abbey was dissolved by Henry VIII in 1539, the abbey church was purchased by the people of the town for £400, to use as a parish church. It became St Albans Cathedral in 1877. The photograph on page 40 shows the imposing west front of St Albans Cathedral in 1921, following the completion of its restoration thirty years before. It gives a good impression of the extraordinary length of the church, and an idea of the effect this must have had on the many pilgrims who travelled there in the Middle Ages to worship at the shrine of St Alban.

RECIPE

BRUSSELS SPROUTS WITH CHESTNUTS AND BACON

Chestnuts were introduced into Britain by the Romans. Fresh chestnuts are available in late autumn and winter, just in time for Christmas. In this recipe they are teamed with Brussels sprouts, a traditional part of the Christmas Day meal, as a link between the Roman origins of the city of St Albans and St Alban, the first Christian martyr. Peeling fresh chestnuts is a fiddly job but their flavour is worth the effort. If you don't want the bother of peeling fresh chestnuts, vacuum-packed peeled chestnuts or chestnuts in cans or jars are often available in supermarkets at Christmas time.

> 350g/12oz fresh chestnuts
> 675g/1½ lbs Brussels sprouts
> 300ml/ ½ pint chicken or vegetable stock
> 25g/1oz butter
> 115g/4oz streaky bacon, de-rinded and cut into
> small thin strips (optional)
> Salt and freshly ground black pepper

Use a sharp knife to cut a cross on the flat side of each chestnut, then cook them in boiling salted water for 5 minutes. Drain, then peel off both the tough outer shell and the finer inner one whilst the chestnuts are hot (this can be done in advance of cooking the meal, if necessary). Put the stock in a pan and bring to the boil. Add the chestnuts, reduce heat to low and simmer very gently for 10-15 minutes, until the chestnuts are tender. Drain and keep warm. Meanwhile, cook the Brussels sprouts in boiling salted water for 8-10 minutes, until they are tender. Drain thoroughly and keep warm. Melt the butter in a pan, add the chopped bacon and cook for a few minutes until the bacon is crisp. Add the sprouts and chestnuts, and season to taste with freshly ground black pepper. Toss the vegetables in the melted butter to coat them, then serve. (If you don't want to use bacon, just toss the vegetables and butter together over a high heat for a few seconds to coat them, season to taste and serve.)

RECIPE

TROUT WITH ALMONDS

Trout, eels and crayfish used to be caught in abundance in many Hertfordshire rivers, such as the Ver, the Gade and the Mimram. In the mid 17th century Izaak Walton, author of 'The Compleat Angler', loved to fish in the River Lea near Hoddesdon, regarding it as one of his favourite fishing spots. He stayed at The Thatched House Inn at Hoddesdon (which stood on the site of what is now 124-128 High Street), which he described as 'an honest alehouse, where we shall find a cleanly room, lavender at the windows and twenty ballads stuck about the walls'. The Thatched House Inn is now gone, but trout are still caught in the Lea and other rivers in the county. In 1967, 'Trencherman' reported in 'Hertfordshire Countryside' magazine that the cost of a main course of two trout cooked in butter with almonds was 11s 6d (62p) at the George and Dragon Inn at Codicote in the Mimram valley. Sadly, this dish will cost a few more pence to serve up nowadays! This amount will feed four people, so increase the quantities for more.

> 4 whole trout, gutted and cleaned, with the heads left on
> 4 tablespoonfuls plain flour
> Salt and pepper
> 115g/4oz butter
> 50g/2oz flaked almonds
> Juice of half a lemon
> Cut the remaining half of the lemon into thin slices, to garnish

Mix the flour with salt and pepper and use it to coat the fish on both sides. Melt 75g/3oz of the butter in a large frying pan. Slide in the trout and cook for about 15 minutes, turning halfway through cooking time, until they are golden brown on both sides and cooked through. Drain the trout and keep warm on a serving dish. Clean the pan, then melt the remaining butter in it. Add the flaked almonds and fry carefully until they are lightly browned, stirring frequently. Stir in the lemon juice and heat gently, then pour the sauce over the trout in the serving dish. Garnish with the lemon slices and serve.

RICKMANSWORTH, CANAL BOATS 1921 70506x

This shows part of the Grand Junction Canal at Rickmansworth, re-designated the Grand Union Canal in 1929 when it was linked up with seven other canals, and portrays an excellent example of co-operation between barges on the busy canal network. The two central barges have been lashed together in order to bypass those moored alongside the canal bank. The barge horse of one of the craft is being led forward along the towpath, and will soon be harnessed up again (the other barge horse is just out of shot in this view, a section of a larger photograph, waiting for the manoeuvre to be completed). One of the bargees has summoned his wife or daughter to take the tiller, whilst he stands on the bow ready to cast the towing line ashore. Note the bargee woman on the second barge from the left, still wearing a traditional bonnet even in the 1920s. In later years, from 1947 until 1980, L Rose & Co used the canal to transport raw lime juice from London to Boxmoor Wharf at Hemel Hempstead, where it was unloaded and sent to Rose's St Albans' works for bottling into Rose's Lime Juice Cordial.

RECIPE

HERTFORDSHIRE ROLLED BEEF

675g/1½ lb braising steak, in one piece,
    preferably about 2cms (¾ inch) thick
115g/4oz fresh breadcrumbs
50g/2oz shredded suet
1 teaspoonful finely chopped fresh parsley
1 teaspoonful finely chopped fresh sage leaves
    (or half a teaspoonful chopped dried sage)
Salt and freshly ground black pepper
1 egg, beaten
300ml/ ½ pint beef or vegetable stock
1 tablespoonful plain flour or cornflower to make the gravy

Pre-heat the oven to 180°C/350°F/Gas Mark 4. Mix together the breadcrumbs, suet, parsley, and sage, and season to taste with salt and pepper. Bind together into a thick paste with the beaten egg. Lay out the meat flat and spread it with the stuffing mixture. Roll up the meat like a Swiss roll, and tie with kitchen string in several places, to secure it firmly. Put the meat roll in a deep ovenproof dish and pour in the stock. Cover the dish with its lid and bake in the pre-heated oven for about 2 hours, until the meat is tender. Check from time to time to make sure there is plenty of liquid left in the dish, and top up with a little more stock if necessary – you will need about 300ml (½ pint) left when the meat is cooked, to make the gravy. When cooked, take out the meat and keep it hot. In a saucepan, blend one tablespoonful of plain flour or cornflour into two tablespoonfuls taken from the cooking liquid in the dish. Gradually add the remaining liquid and bring to the boil, stirring continuously, to make a thick gravy. Reduce the heat and allow the gravy to simmer for one minute, still stirring. Check for seasoning, then serve the gravy with the meat, cut into slices across the roll.

RECIPE

TOAD IN THE HOLE WITH BRAUGHING SAUSAGES

The Braughing Sausage is named after the village of Braughing in east Hertfordshire, where the recipe was devised by a local butcher, Douglas White, in 1954, and sold from his shop at 15 Green End. It proved so popular that it soon became one of Hertfordshire's food legends. A few years ago D White's Butchers was purchased by Musk's of Newmarket, makers of the equally famous Newmarket Sausage. The Braughing Sausage is now produced at the Musk's factory in Newmarket, but it continues to be made to Douglas White's exact recipe. Braughing Sausages are still sold from the original D White's Butcher's shop at Braughing, and are also available online from www.braughingsausage.com. They are just the sort of meaty, well-flavoured sausages you need to use for this recipe.

> 450g/1 lb Braughing Sausages
> 175g/6oz plain flour
> A pinch of salt
> 2 eggs
> 600ml/1 pint milk and water mixed
> 15g/ ½ oz lard or dripping

Make the batter 1 hour before you start cooking the dish. Put the flour in a bowl with the salt, make a well in the centre and break in the eggs. Beat them into the flour, gradually adding the milk and water to make a smooth, creamy batter. Beat it well, then leave to stand for 1 hour. Pre-heat the oven to 220°C/425°F/Gas Mark 7. Melt the lard or dripping in a frying pan and brown the sausages nicely all over (this gives a better flavour than cooking the sausages in the oven). Pour the fat and sausages into a roasting tin. Place the tin in the oven for a few minutes to heat through, then remove from the oven, pour in the prepared batter and replace the tin in the oven. When the batter is nicely puffed up, reduce the oven temperature to 190°C/375°F/Gas Mark 5, and continue cooking until it is well-risen and golden brown – the total cooking time from start to finish should be 35-40 minutes.

In the early 1600s, King James I (1566-1625) had a hunting lodge-cum-summer palace built at Royston in Hertfordshire. The king was an inveterate huntsman, and nearby Therfield Heath, south-west of the town, provided him with the thrill of the chase – the king actually prohibited anyone else from hunting game within 16 miles of Royston, to protect his sport. The royal buildings in Royston fell into disrepair after the Civil War, but part of the palace still stands in Kneesworth Street in the town, a building with two tall chimneys known as the Old Palace. The building next door to it was originally the palace's kitchen. Behind the palace were the royal dog kennels where the hounds were kept, remembered today in the byway in Royston called Dog Kennel Lane. King James I and his courtiers spent a great deal of time in Royston, hunting, feasting and generally enjoying themselves, so much so that the local people could not cope with the demands of supplying them with food and drink. One evening someone tied a note to the collar of the king's favourite dog, Jowler, for him to see, which read: 'Good Mr Jowler, we pray you to speak to the King (for he hears you every day and so he doth not us) that it will please His Majesty to go back to London, for else the country will be undone; all our provision is spent already and we are not able to entertain him longer.'

(Quoted in 'A History of Hertfordshire' by Tony Rook, Philimore & Co. Ltd, 1984.)

RECIPE

VENISON CASSEROLE

Nowadays anyone in Hertfordshire can eat like a king, with venison from the National Trust's Ashbridge Estate, near Berkhamsted, available from Gade Valley Game at Great Gaddesden, near Hemel Hempstead. A good way of cooking venison is in a casserole.

> 1kg/2 lb 4oz venison braising steak, cut into cubes
> 2 tablespoonfuls plain flour, seasoned
> 50g/2oz butter
> 2 tablespoonfuls oil
> 2 onions, peeled and thinly sliced
> 1 clove of garlic, peeled and finely chopped
> 600ml/1 pint stock
> 150ml/ ¼ pint red wine
> 1 tablespoonful tomato purée
> 225g/8oz carrots
> 115g/4oz mushrooms
> 2 dessertspoonfuls redcurrant jelly
> Salt and freshly ground black pepper

Pre-heat the oven to 180°C/350°F/Gas Mark 4. Toss the cubes of venison in seasoned flour so all sides are covered. Melt half the butter and oil together in a flameproof casserole. Fry the venison, a few cubes at a time, until all sides are browned. Put the browned meat to one side and keep warm. Melt the remaining butter and oil in the casserole, add the sliced onions and cook gently for about 10 minutes, until they are soft and transparent, then add the garlic. Stir in the remaining seasoned flour and cook for 1-2 minutes. Add the tomato purée, and then the stock and the red wine, a little at a time, stirring continually. Increase the heat and bring the sauce to the boil, constantly stirring as it thickens. Season to taste with salt and pepper, then add the sliced carrots and mushrooms and the browned venison pieces. Put the lid on the casserole and cook in the pre-heated oven for about 1½ - 2 hours. Stir the redcurrant jelly into the casserole 10 minutes before serving. This casserole is even better if it is made the day before needed, and reheated in the oven before serving.

RECIPE

PORK PLUGGER

This traditional savoury steamed suet pudding filled with chopped bacon and onions is called Pork Plugger around Bishop's Stortford.

175g/6oz self-raising flour
115g/4oz shredded suet
Salt and freshly ground black pepper
About 6 tablespoonfuls of water
2 tablespoonfuls of chopped fresh parsley
225g/8oz unsmoked bacon rashers, de-rinded
    and chopped into pieces
225g/8oz onion, peeled and sliced
Half a teaspoonful soft brown sugar
1 tablespoonful of chopped fresh sage leaves
    (or 1 dessertspoonful of dried sage)
A small amount of stock
1 tablespoonful cooking oil

Melt the butter in a pan, add the sliced onion and sprinkle over the brown sugar. Fry the onion over a gentle heat until it is soft and lightly browned, stirring occasionally so it doesn't stick and burn. Remove the cooked onion from the pan and put to one side. Gently fry the bacon pieces in the same pan until the fat is starting to run and they are cooked through, then add the onion back to the pan and season to taste with plenty of freshly ground black pepper and a little salt, if needed – the bacon will already be salty. Mix together, then leave to cool whilst you make the suet pastry.

Sieve the flour into a bowl, season with salt and pepper and add the parsley and the suet. Mix together with enough cold water to form a soft dough. Knead the dough for a few minutes, then roll it out on a floured surface into a rectangle about 1cm (½ inch) thick.

Spread the dough with the bacon and onion mixture, leaving 1cm (½ inch) around the edges, and sprinkle over a small amount of stock, to moisten the mixture. Scatter the sage over the filling. Roll it all up like a Swiss roll. Wet the ends lightly, and pinch the edges of the dough together well to seal them. Wrap the roll very loosely in a piece of buttered, pleated greaseproof paper and then a further piece of pleated foil (this allows room for the pudding to expand during cooking), and seal the seams and ends of the wrapping firmly. Fill the bottom half of a large steamer or fish kettle with water and bring it to the boil. Put in the roll (curve it to fit if necessary), cover the pan with its lid and boil for about 3 hours, topping up the pan with more boiling water as necessary, so it does not boil dry. When cooked, lift out the roll, unwrap and place on an ovenproof serving dish in a pre-heated oven for 10 minutes to finish, at 180°C/350°F/Gas Mark 4. Serve cut into slices, with potatoes and root vegetables like turnips, carrots, parsnips or swede.

BISHOP'S STORTFORD, THE CORN EXCHANGE 1903 49757

TRING, HIGH STREET 1897 T81001

This photograph shows Tring's High Street in 1897, decorated with flags to celebrate Queen Victoria's Diamond Jubilee – 60 years on the throne. Tring used to be famous for Tring Dumplings, which had a savoury meat filling at one end, usually pork or bacon, and a sweet filling at the other, made either from jam, or fruit in season such as apples, with the two halves separated by a wedge of pastry. Tring Dumplings were made by the wives and mothers of men working as agricultural labourers for them to take into the fields to be consumed for 'beaver', a Hertfordshire name for a snack eaten at work. They were made with suet crust pastry and the traditional way of cooking them was to boil them, wrapped in a pudding cloth. Any leftover pastry was often made into small balls, about the size of a walnut, and dropped into the simmering water to cook at the same time, which would take about half an hour. They were known as 'swimmers', and when they were cooked they were scooped out, put on a plate and given to children as a treat, to eat hot with honey, treacle or jam.

**MUCH HADHAM, MAIN STREET
1899** 44880x

RECIPE

PLUM AND WALNUT CRUMBLE

The famous Rivers Nursery at Sawbridgeworth, founded in 1725 by John Rivers and closed in 1985, was where many new varieties of fruit were developed, including over 20 different species of plum, such as 'Czar' a popular culinary variety with a sharp flavour, and the delicious 'Mallard', a red sweet plum. Celebrate the proud place of the plum in Hertfordshire's food history with this scrumptious dessert, where plums are teamed with chopped walnuts. Walnut trees grow well in the rich soil of the many river valleys of the county. In 'The History of Hertfordshire describing the County and its Ancient Monuments', an important early history published in 1728, the author Nathaniel Salmon quaintly referred to the magnificent oaks, elms and walnut trees of Hertfordshire as the county's 'glorious vegetables'.

> 1kg/2 lb plums, halved and stoned
> 75g/3oz walnut pieces
> 75g/3oz butter or margarine, diced
> 175g/6oz plain flour
> 175g/6oz demerara sugar

Pre-heat the oven to 180°C/350°F/Gas Mark 4. Spread the nuts on a baking sheet and place in the oven for 8-10 minutes, until they are evenly coloured.

Butter a 1.2 litre (2 pint) ovenproof dish. Put the plums into the dish and stir in the walnut pieces and half the demerara sugar. Rub the butter or margarine into the flour until the mixture resembles coarse breadcrumbs. Stir in the remaining sugar and continue to rub in until fine crumbs are formed. Cover the fruit with the crumb mixture and press it down lightly. Bake in the pre-heated oven for about 45 minutes, until the top is crisp and golden brown and the fruit is tender. Serve with custard, cream or ice-cream.

CROXLEY GREEN
THE OLD TREE
1897 39688x

HATFIELD, HATFIELD HOUSE c1965 H254062

Hatfield House was built in the early 17th century by Robert Cecil (1563-1612), first Earl of Salisbury and Chief Minister to King James I. However, when Samuel Pepys visited Hatfield House in July 1661, he was more impressed by the huge gooseberries grown in its garden than the magnificent Jacobean mansion, recording in his famous diary that at Hatfield '…I met with Mr. Looker, my Lord's gardener…, who showed me the house, the chappell with brave pictures, and, above all, the gardens, such as I never saw in all my life; nor so good flowers, nor so great gooseberrys, as big as nutmegs…'. Before Robert Cecil built Hatfield House, an earlier building called Hatfield Palace stood on the site. This was the childhood home of two of Henry VIII's children, Princess Elizabeth and Prince Edward, and Elizabeth was also imprisoned there in 1558 after being held in the Tower of London on suspicion of plotting against her elder sister, Queen Mary I. Only part of Hatfield Palace exists now, but the oak tree still stands in its park beneath which Elizabeth was sitting when she was told of her sister Mary's death and her accession to the throne as Queen Elizabeth I.

RECIPE

GOOSEBERRY AND ELDERFLOWER SYLLABUBS

This recipe recalls the gooseberries at Hatfield House that so impressed Samuel Pepys. It makes a creamy dessert like the syllabubs that were popular in Tudor times, and which might well have been enjoyed by Princess Elizabeth at Hatfield Palace. Elderflower cordial is an ingredient of this dessert and is available in most supermarkets, but use white wine instead if you prefer. This quantity should make six servings.

300g/10oz fresh gooseberries
150g/5oz caster sugar
300ml/10 fl oz double cream
Finely grated zest of one lemon
150ml/5 fl oz elderflower cordial (or white wine if preferred)

Place the gooseberries in a heavy saucepan with half the sugar and 2 tablespoonfuls of water. Cook over medium heat until the sugar has dissolved and the liquid is bubbling, then reduce the heat, cover the pan and cook gently at a low simmer for about 20 minutes or until the gooseberries are stewed and soft, stirring occasionally so they don't stick. Remove from the heat and leave to cool for a few minutes. Reserve 6 gooseberries for decoration, then process the rest in a blender or liquidizer to form a puree. Place all but one tablespoonful of the gooseberry purée in six dessert dishes or tall glasses, and leave to cool.

Whip together the cream, the lemon zest and remaining sugar, gradually adding in the elderflower cordial (or wine) and the reserved gooseberry purée when the mixture is beginning to thicken. Carry on whipping until soft peaks form, and the mixture is thick and light, but not stiff. Divide the mixture between the dishes or glasses, on top of the gooseberry purée. Decorate each serving with one of the reserved gooseberries. Cover with cling film and place the desserts in the fridge to chill before serving.

BERKHAMSTED, HIGH STREET c1955 B407018

Berkhamsted has a place in Hertfordshire's food history as the birthplace of the popular cooking apple variety now known as Lane's Prince Albert. The original Lane's Prince Albert apple tree was in the garden of a house called The Homestead at 250 High Street in the town, which was demolished in 1958, along with the tree. Thomas Squire, who lived at The Homestead, often experimented with plants and cuttings. On 26 July 1841 he planted out a small apple tree after cheering Queen Victoria and Prince Albert, the Prince Consort, as they drove through the town. Thomas named the tree the 'Victoria and Albert', and in due course it bore excellent fruit. The new apple variety was marketed commercially by the Henry Lane & Son nursery business in Berkhamsted, renamed as 'Lane's Prince Albert'. It is a late-cropping cooking apple with a lovely, sharp-tasting fruit. The grain is fine and does not disintegrate in the oven, so it is an ideal apple for baking whole, as in the recipe on the opposite page.

RECIPE

BAKED APPLES WITH BUTTERSCOTCH SAUCE

Try to use Lane's Prince Albert Apples if possible, but otherwise any good cooking apple will be fine for this recipe. Serves 6.

> 6 large cooking apples, cored but left whole, and unpeeled
> 115g/4oz sultanas
> 2 tablespoonfuls brandy
> 4 level tablespoonfuls soft brown sugar
> 2 tablespoonfuls apple juice
>
> <u>For the sauce:</u>
> 115g/4oz butter
> 115g/4oz soft brown sugar
> 2 tablespoonfuls golden syrup
> 2 tablespoonfuls black treacle
> 4 tablespoonfuls brandy
> 300ml/ ½ pint double cream
> 115g/4oz chopped and toasted hazelnuts

Pre-heat the oven to 220°C/425°F/Gas Mark 7. Soak the sultanas in the brandy and set aside for 10 minutes, then stuff the core cavity of each apple with equal amounts. Place the apples in a roasting tin, and sprinkle over the brown sugar and apple juice. Bake in the pre-heated oven for 15-20 minutes or until they are soft.

Whilst the apples are baking, make the sauce. Melt the butter, soft brown sugar, golden syrup and treacle in a heavy-based pan, stirring continually. When the sugar has dissolved and the mixture is bubbling, stir in the brandy and cream. Bring back to the boil, then set aside until the apples are ready. Serve the baked apples with the sauce poured over them, topped with a sprinkling of toasted chopped hazelnuts.

STEVENAGE, A SHOP IN HIGH STREET 1899   44259x

A number of Hertfordshire food traditions are associated with Easter,
the most important Christian religious festival. Easter commemorates
the crucifixion of Jesus Christ on 'Good Friday', then celebrates
Christ's resurrection on Easter Sunday. The 40 day period leading
up to Easter is known as Lent. It begins on Ash Wednesday and
concludes on 'Holy Saturday' of Easter, the day after Good Friday, at
the end of 'Holy Week'. The Sunday at the beginning of Holy Week is
known as Palm Sunday in memory of Christ's entry into Jerusalem
before his arrest and trial, when people strewed his path with palm
branches to honour him, but until quite recent times it was known as
Fig Sunday in Hertfordshire, as tradition maintains that Christ ate figs
on this day. It was the custom in many parts of the county, especially
north Hertfordshire, to eat figs on Fig Sunday, perhaps cooked in a
boiled suet pudding or stewed and eaten with rice pudding. Another
traditional Hertfordshire dessert for Fig Sunday was fig jelly, made
from the juice of stewed figs.

RECIPE

FIG JELLY

250g/9oz dried figs
50g/2oz sugar
600ml/1 pint water
1 sachet of powdered gelatine
(enough to set 600ml/1 pint of liquid)

Put the figs, sugar and water into a saucepan. Bring to the boil, stirring occasionally until the sugar dissolves, then reduce the heat to low, cover the pan and stew the figs at a gentle simmer for one hour. When cooked, strain the liquid through a sieve and measure it. You need 600ml (1 pint) liquid – make it up to this with boiling water if necessary.

Put 120ml/4fl oz of the hot stewing liquid into a jug or small bowl, and sprinkle on the powdered gelatine. Stir with a fork until it is all dissolved, then pour the mixture into the rest of the fig liquid and stir well. Rinse out a jelly mould or glass dish with cold water, then pour in the fig liquid. Cover and leave in the fridge overnight, for the jelly to set.

The leftover cooked figs can be cut up and eaten as they are (traditionally they were eaten with rice pudding), or used to make something else, perhaps a boiled suet Fig Pudding if you wish.

SHROVING

'I've come a shrov'in
Vor a little pancaik...'

Shrove Tuesday is the day before Ash Wednesday, the first day of Lent
(see page 36), and was traditionally the day for 'shriving' – confessing
sins and asking forgiveness – before Lent began. Lent was a period of
religious fasting and dietary austerity in the past, when eggs, butter,
meat and certain other foods were not allowed to be eaten. This is
the origin of what we now call Pancake Day, when making pancakes
on Shrove Tuesday was a way of using up some 'forbidden foods' in
the larder before Lent began. In Hoddesdon in Hertfordshire it used
to be the custom for the old curfew bell, known as 'the Pancake Bell',
to be rung at 4 o'clock on Shrove Tuesday morning to tell people
they could start making and eating pancakes, then rung at 8 o'clock
in the evening to tell them to stop cooking and extinguish their fires.
A custom known as 'shroving' also took place on Shrove Tuesday
in many parts of the country in the past, when children would go
around 'begging with menaces' for treats, rather like children do at
Halloween nowadays. This shroving rhyme recited by children in the
Hertfordshire village of Baldock was recorded in 1894:

'I've come a shrov'in
Vor a little pancaik
A bit of bread of your baikin;
Or a little truckle cheese o' you maikin':
If you gie me a little, I'll ax no more,
If you don't gi me nothing, I'll rattle your door.'

Nowadays Pancake Day is celebrated in Hertfordshire with pancake
races in several towns, and Hitchin holds an annual Pancake
Festival which raises money for local charities as well as being an
entertaining feature in the town's calendar.

RECIPE

QUICK AND EASY SPICED DOUGHNUTS

When the children of Baldock were out shroving in the past, some of the treats they received might have been small fried cakes, or doughnuts. In 1832 William Horne recorded in 'The Year Book of Daily Information and Recreation' that 'At Baldock in Hertfordshire, Shrove Tuesday is long counted of by the juveniles, by whom it is known as "Dough-Nut Day", it being usual for the "mothers" to make good store of small cakes fried in hog's lard, placed over the fire in a brass kettle or skillet, called "dough-nuts", wherewith the "younger fry" are plenteously regaled'. These small doughnuts are easy to make, and will be just as popular with modern children.

500g/1 lb 2oz plain flour
1 heaped teaspoonful baking powder
1 teaspoonful ground cinnamon
75g/3oz butter, cut into pieces
75g/3oz caster sugar
1 egg, beaten

250ml/9 fl oz milk
Vegetable oil for frying
175g/6oz extra sugar, for coating the doughnuts
1 teaspoonful extra ground cinnamon

Sieve the flour, baking powder and cinnamon into a bowl and rub in the butter. Mix in the sugar. Beat the egg and milk together, then pour into the flour mixture. Combine it all together to form a ball of soft dough. Roll out the dough on a floured surface to about 1cm (½ inch) thick and cut out rounds of dough about 6cms (2 inches) in diameter (or form pieces of dough into balls about the size of a golf ball, if preferred). Mix the extra sugar and cinnamon together in a bowl. Heat the oil in a deep fryer or frying pan and fry the doughnuts in batches for about 30 seconds on each side, until they are crisp and golden brown. Drain each doughnut on kitchen paper, then roll in the sugar and cinnamon mixture whilst still hot, to coat it all over. These are especially nice whilst still hot and crisp.

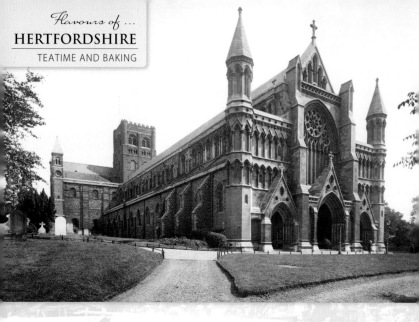

ST ALBANS, THE CATHEDRAL AND ABBEY CHURCH 1921 70455

Another food item associated with Easter is the Hot Cross Bun, which is traditionally eaten on Good Friday. This spiced, fruited bun is decorated with a cross on the top, usually made of glazed sugar or thin strips of dough, which commemorates the crucifixion of Jesus Christ on this day. It is claimed that the association of Hot Cross Buns with Easter derives from Hertfordshire, when in 1361 a Father Thomas Rockliffe of St Albans Abbey (now St Albans Cathedral) handed out sweet, spiced buns to the poor after the Good Friday Mass, which he had decorated with a cross cut into the top of the dough. Hot Cross Buns decorated this way, known as 'Albans', are sold in the café at St Albans Cathedral during Holy Week – the last week of Lent, leading up to Good Friday. Freshly-baked home-made hot cross buns are delicious, and not difficult to make. The recipe on the opposite page decorates them St Albans-style, with the cross cut into the dough. The amount in this recipe makes 12 buns, which are best eaten on the day they are made.

RECIPE

ST ALBANS HOT CROSS BUNS

450g/1 lb strong white breadmaking flour
200ml/7 fl oz milk
1 teaspoonful salt
3 teaspoonfuls fast acting dried yeast
50g/2oz butter, cut into small pieces
1 egg, beaten
50g/2oz caster sugar
75g/3oz currants
25g/1oz chopped mixed peel
1 teaspoonful ground mixed spice
1 teaspoonful ground cinnamon
Half a teaspoonful ground nutmeg
<u>For the glaze:</u>
2 tablespoonfuls extra caster sugar
2 tablespoonfuls extra milk

Warm the milk to hand hot. Sift the flour, salt and spices into a large bowl. Rub in the butter. Stir in the fast acting dried yeast, then the sugar, currants and peel. Stir in the beaten egg with the warmed milk. Combine it all to form a workable dough, and knead on a floured surface for 10 minutes until it is smooth and no longer sticky. Place the dough in a greased bowl, cover with a damp cloth, or place the bowl inside a polythene bag, and leave in a warm place for one hour for the dough to rise. Turn out the dough onto a floured surface, knock it back, and knead gently for a minute. Divide the dough into 12 pieces and shape into round buns. Place on a greased baking sheet, cover and leave to rise again for 30 minutes.

Pre-heat the oven to 190°C/375°F/Gas Mark 5. Cut a deep cross with a sharp knife across each bun. Bake the buns for 15 minutes, until risen and golden brown. Make the glaze by dissolving the sugar in the milk. Remove the buns from the oven and brush with two coatings of glaze whilst they are hot. Transfer to a wire rack to cool.

Until the mid 19th century, the making of pillow lace was a thriving cottage craft in many towns and villages of west Hertfordshire. With gaily-beaded bobbins, women worked on pillows to which pricked parchment or cardboard patterns were attached, glittering with pins to make a framework for the linen threads that were wound about them to make the lace. The lacemakers often learned their trade as children in 'lace schools', where they recited 'tells', or 'chants', to help them learn the patterns. St Catherine of Alexandria was the patron saint of spinners and lacemakers, and in the lacemaking towns and villages of Hertfordshire of the past, lacemakers and the children attending lace schools used to take St Catherine's Day, or 'Cattern Day' – 25th November – as a holiday. They called this 'Keeping Cattern' ('Cattern' being a corruption of 'Catherine'), and called at neighbours' houses, requesting refreshment; 'wigs', small, slightly sweet yeasted buns flavoured with caraway seeds, and 'hot pot' (warm beer containing beaten eggs and rum) were traditional fare on Cattern Day.

Wigs (or wiggs) were popular all over the country in the past. They were usually eaten freshly made, whilst still warm, with ale and cheese. William Ellis of Little Gaddesden, the 18th-century farmer and writer on country matters, used to give them to his farm workers at harvest time. In his book 'The Country Housewife's Family Companion' of 1750 he records that 'Wigs to make for harvestmen' were baked at the entrance to the oven "for about half an Hour; and this we generally do about six o'Clock in the Evening, that they may be hot against the Men come home to Supper from reaping, when we toss one of these large Wigs to each Man for his dipping it in a Bowl of Ale, which serves for an agreeable cooling Supper with Cheese or other Things". He also tells us that he used to give wigs to his men for their 'beaver victuals', the snack that they ate whilst working in the fields.

RECIPE

WIGS

Wigs are small yeasted buns rather like bread rolls, but lighter and richer. They were traditionally flavoured with caraway seeds, which were much used British cookery from the 17th century to the mid-20th century as a flavouring for cakes, breads, buns and biscuits. Wigs were usually served warm from the oven and eaten with ale and cheese in the past, but these savoury buns would also be good served with soup.

> 450g/1 lb plain flour
> 50g/2oz soft brown sugar
> A pinch of salt
> 1 teaspoonful caraway seeds
> 3 teaspoonfuls fast-acting dried yeast
> 300ml/ ½ pint milk
> 50g/2oz butter
> 1 egg

Put the flour, sugar, salt and caraway seeds in a large mixing bowl, and stir in the dried yeast. Warm the milk and melt the butter in it, then leave to cool for a few minutes. When the milk mixture has cooled a little, beat the egg into it, then add to the dry ingredients and mix to form a soft dough. Knead the dough for about five minutes until it is smooth and elastic, then put it in a greased bowl, cover with a cloth or put the bowl inside a polythene bag, and leave in a warm place for about 1½ hours until the dough has doubled in size. Divide the dough into about 20 small pieces and shape them into buns. Place the buns on greased baking sheets, well spaced out, and leave to rise again in a warm place for about 30 minutes, then bake in a pre-heated oven for about 15-20 minutes (200°C/400°F/Gas Mark 6).

RECIPE

PUCKERIDGE FARM BREAD

This easy recipe for a fruited tea bread comes from Puckeridge, a village in east Hertfordshire between Bishop's Stortford and Stevenage. When making this, remember to soak the sultanas in (milkless) tea in good time before you need them – this makes the fruit lovely and juicy, resulting in a deliciously moist and tasty tea bread.

> 175g/6oz sultanas
> 115g/4oz golden caster sugar, or soft brown sugar
> 250ml/ 9fl oz hot milkless tea
> 225g/8oz self-raising flour (either white or brown
>   self-raising flour works well in this)
> 1 egg, beaten

Put the sultanas in a bowl, add the hot, milkless tea, cover the bowl and leave to soak for at least 5 hours, preferably overnight.

Pre-heat the oven to 180°C/350°F/Gas Mark 4. Grease a 450g/1 lb loaf tin.

Put the flour and sugar into a large mixing bowl. Stir in the sultanas and the remaining soaking liquid, and then the beaten egg. Mix it all together well, then pour the mixture into the loaf tin. Bake just below the centre of the pre-heated oven for about 45-55 minutes, until it is well risen and golden, and firm to the touch – check the cake towards the end of the cooking time, and bake for a little longer if it looks like it can take it. Leave in the tin for 15 minutes to settle before turning out.

This can be eaten either warm or cold, cut into slices and spread with butter.

RECIPE

CHERRY TURNOVERS

Cherry orchards were once a common sight in south-west Hertfordshire, and the county was famous for the Hertfordshire Black and dark Carroon (or Kerroon) cherry varieties. The village of Frithsden near Berkhamsted is said to be where 'Cherry Bounce' was invented, a liqueur made by steeping cherries and sugar in spirits such as vodka, brandy, rum or whisky for about 4 months. Frithsden is also claimed to be where the Cherry Turnover originated, a delicious way of eating lovely fresh cherries. The cherries for this recipe must be really ripe, when they are juicy and full of flavour.

> 450g/1 lb fresh, ripe cherries
> 75g/3oz soft brown or caster sugar
> 225g/8oz shortcrust pastry
> A little milk, to finish
> A little extra caster sugar, to finish

Pre-heat the oven to 200°C/400°F/Gas Mark 6. Grease a couple of baking trays and line with dampened greaseproof or baking paper. Stalk and stone the cherries, either with a stoner or by cutting them in half to remove the kernels. Roll out the pastry and cut it into 15cm (6 inch) rounds. Heap the centre of each pastry round with cherries, leaving a good margin round the edge, and sprinkle the cherries liberally with sugar. Damp the edges of each pastry round by brushing it with water, then bring up one half of each round over the filling to the other side, to make a half-moon shape, like a pasty. Seal the edges well by pinching them together with your fingers, then crimp along the rounded edge with a fork. Brush each turnover with a little milk and sprinkle with a little caster sugar. Bake in the pre-heated oven for about 25 minutes. Place on a wire rack and dredge with more sugar. These can be eaten eat hot or cold.

RICKMANSWORTH, HIGH STREET 1921
70500

HITCHIN, MARKET PLACE 1922   71893

Hitchin has held a weekly market since at least the 12th century. Livestock and local produce comprised a large proportion of the goods traded at Hitchin's busy markets in the past: horses, cattle, sheep, pigs and fowl, as well as grain, vegetables and dairy products, leatherwork and straw plait. For many centuries the Market Place at Hitchin was also where local miscreants were punished, and in 1774 Elizabeth Parr was publicly whipped there for the theft of nutmeg. Nutmeg features as a prominent ingredient in the recipe on the opposite page for Rich Cake, an adaptation of one included in 'Take 6 Carrots, 4 Heads of Celery, 8 Large Onions', published by Hitchin Historical Society in 1994, a collection of recipes edited and adapted by Maya Pieris from old recipe books and papers of the wealthy and influential Wilshere family, which was prominent in Hitchin in the 18th and 19th centuries. The recipe given here has been adapted to make a smaller cake than in the original version, which called for 24 eggs!

RECIPE

RICH CAKE

225g/8oz butter or margarine
115g/4oz dark brown sugar
4 eggs, separated
75g/3oz blanched flaked almonds
Half a nutmeg, finely grated (or 2 teaspoonfuls ground nutmeg)
75g/3oz chopped mixed peel
350g/12oz currants, or a mixture of currants and raisins
225g/8oz plain flour
100ml/3½ fl oz medium sweet sherry, or sweet white wine

Pre-heat the oven to 170°C/325°F/Gas Mark 3. Grease and line a deep cake tin 22-24cms (9 inches) in diameter. Cream the butter and sugar together. Mix in the beaten egg yolks, then beat in the almonds, nutmeg, peel and dried fruit. Beat in the flour in batches, alternating with the sherry or wine. In a separate bowl, whisk the egg whites until they are stiff. Use a large metal spoon to fold the egg whites gently but thoroughly into the cake mixture. Turn the mixture into the prepared tin and smooth the top, hollowing the centre slightly. Bake in the centre of the pre-heated oven for 1½ - 2 hours, covering the top of the cake with foil or kitchen paper if it is browning too quickly. Test with a knife or metal skewer to see if the cake is done – it should come out clean when the cake is cooked, and the top of the cake should feel just firm to the touch. Cook the cake for a little longer if it needs it. After baking, leave the cake in the tin for 30 minutes, then turn out on to a wire rack, remove the lining paper and leave to cool. Store in an airtight container, or wrapped in greaseproof paper and foil. This improves with being kept for a couple of days before eating, to allow the flavours to develop.

WATFORD, HIGH STREET 1961 W40048

RECIPE

TEWIN APPLE CAKE

Until the mid 20th century, there were hundreds of small-scale orchards around Hertfordshire. Most of those traditional orchards have now been swallowed up by housing or are used for other agricultural purposes, but in recent years the Hertfordshire Orchards Initiative (HOI) has been working hard to preserve those that remain, so their heritage and wildlife value can be preserved for the future. HOI runs a number of Apple Day events around the county each year, including one at the Stanley Lord Orchard at Shenley Park near Watford; this historic orchard is planted with over 120 varieties of apple trees, with an emphasis on species that originate from Hertfordshire or the surrounding area. There are also a number of Community Orchards around the county nowadays, including one at the village of Tewin, near Welwyn Garden City, where this recipe originates from. This unusual but delicious dish is a cross between an apple roly poly and a lardy cake. It is made of bread dough rolled up like a Swiss roll around an apple filling, and the bottom half gets a sticky toffee coating whilst it bakes. It is best eaten hot, fresh from the oven, whilst the outer crust is crispy and gooey.

For the dough:
450g/1 lb plain flour
Half a teaspoonful salt
2 heaped teaspoonfuls of fast acting dried yeast (or a 7g sachet)
115g/4oz butter or margarine, cut into small pieces
300ml/1 pint milk
For the filling:
1 lb cooking apples
115g/4oz softened butter
175g/6oz soft brown sugar
1 teaspoonful ground cinnamon

First, make the dough. Sift the flour and salt into a large bowl. Rub in the butter or margarine until the mixture resembles fine breadcrumbs. Add the dried yeast and stir so it is all well mixed. Gently warm the milk until it is lukewarm, then pour it into a well in the flour mixture and mix it all together to form a dough. Flour your hands and knead the dough for about 5 minutes until it is smooth and elastic. Place the dough in a bowl, cover the bowl with a damp cloth, or place the bowl inside an oiled polythene bag, and leave in a warm place to rise until it has doubled in size, for about one hour. When the dough is risen, turn it out onto a floured surface and knock it back, then knead it again very gently for a minute or so. Roll out the dough on a floured surface to form a rectangle about 1cm (½ inch) thick.

Grease a 1kg (2 lb) loaf tin. Peel and core the apples, and chop them into very small pieces. Mash the softened butter with a fork and spread it all over the dough. Spread the sugar on top of the butter, and then sprinkle the cinnamon evenly over it. Cover with the diced apples, and press the pieces gently into the topping a bit, to firm it all up. Roll up the dough like a Swiss roll and seal the ends by pressing the edges of the dough together firmly. Place the roll – seam side down – in the greased loaf tin, cover and leave in a warm place to 'rest' for 30 minutes.

Pre-heat the oven to 200°C/400°F/Gas Mark 6. Place the cake in the centre of the oven and bake for around 30 minutes, or until it is well risen, with a crispy, light golden crust. Remove the tin from the oven and turn out the cake onto a warmed serving dish, together with any hot sticky sauce that is left in the tin. Cut into slices and serve hot, with cream.

FRANCIS FRITH

PIONEER VICTORIAN PHOTOGRAPHER

Francis Frith, founder of the world-famous photographic archive, was a complex and multi-talented man. A devout Quaker and a highly successful Victorian businessman, he was philosophical by nature and pioneering in outlook. By 1855 he had already established a wholesale grocery business in Liverpool, and sold it for the astonishing sum of £200,000, which is the equivalent today of over £15,000,000. Now in his thirties, and captivated by the new science of photography, Frith set out on a series of pioneering journeys up the Nile and to the Near East.

INTRIGUE AND EXPLORATION

He was the first photographer to venture beyond the sixth cataract of the Nile. Africa was still the mysterious 'Dark Continent', and Stanley and Livingstone's historic meeting was a decade into the future. The conditions for picture taking confound belief. He laboured for hours in his wicker dark-room in the sweltering heat of the desert, while the volatile chemicals fizzed dangerously in their trays. Back in London he exhibited his photographs and was 'rapturously cheered' by members of the Royal Society. His reputation as a photographer was made overnight.

VENTURE OF A LIFE-TIME

By the 1870s the railways had threaded their way across the country, and Bank Holidays and half-day Saturdays had been made obligatory by Act of Parliament. All of a sudden the working man and his family were able to enjoy days out, take holidays, and see a little more of the world.

With typical business acumen, Francis Frith foresaw that these new tourists would enjoy having souvenirs to commemorate their days out. For the next thirty years he travelled the country by train and by pony and trap, producing fine photographs of seaside resorts and beauty spots that were keenly bought by millions of Victorians. These prints were painstakingly pasted into family albums and pored over during the dark nights of winter, rekindling precious memories of summer excursions. Frith's studio was soon supplying retail shops all over the country, and by 1890 F Frith & Co had become the greatest specialist photographic publishing company in the world, with over 2,000 sales outlets, and pioneered the picture postcard.

FRANCIS FRITH'S LEGACY

Francis Frith had died in 1898 at his villa in Cannes, his great project still growing. By 1970 the archive he created contained over a third of a million pictures showing 7,000 British towns and villages.

Frith's legacy to us today is of immense significance and value, for the magnificent archive of evocative photographs he created provides a unique record of change in the cities, towns and villages throughout Britain over a century and more. Frith and his fellow studio photographers revisited locations many times down the years to update their views, compiling for us an enthralling and colourful pageant of British life and character.

We are fortunate that Frith was dedicated to recording the minutiae of everyday life. For it is this sheer wealth of visual data, the painstaking chronicle of changes in dress, transport, street layouts, buildings, housing and landscape that captivates us so much today, offering us a powerful link with the past and with the lives of our ancestors.

Computers have now made it possible for Frith's many thousands of images to be accessed almost instantly. The archive offers every one of us an opportunity to examine the places where we and our families have lived and worked down the years. Its images, depicting our shared past, are now bringing pleasure and enlightenment to millions around the world a century and more after his death.

For further information visit: www.francisfrith.com

INTERIOR DECORATION

Frith's photographs can be seen framed and as giant wall murals in thousands of pubs, restaurants, hotels, banks, retail stores and other public buildings throughout Britain. These provide interesting and attractive décor, generating strong local interest and acting as a powerful reminder of gentler days in our increasingly busy and frenetic world.

FRITH PRODUCTS

All Frith photographs are available as prints and posters in a variety of different sizes and styles. In the UK we also offer a range of other gift and stationery products illustrated with Frith photographs, although many of these are not available for delivery outside the UK – see our web site for more information on the products available for delivery in your country.

THE INTERNET

Over 100,000 photographs of Britain can be viewed and purchased on the Frith web site. The web site also includes memories and reminiscences contributed by our customers, who have personal knowledge of localities and of the people and properties depicted in Frith photographs. If you wish to learn more about a specific town or village you may find these reminiscences fascinating to browse. Why not add your own comments if you think they would be of interest to others? See **www.francisfrith.com**

PLEASE HELP US BRING FRITH'S PHOTOGRAPHS TO LIFE

Our authors do their best to recount the history of the places they write about. They give insights into how particular towns and villages developed, they describe the architecture of streets and buildings, and they discuss the lives of famous people who lived there. But however knowledgeable our authors are, the story they tell is necessarily incomplete.